MANAGING CHANGE

BULLET GUIDE

Hodder Education, 338 Euston Road, London NW1 3BH

Hodder Education is an Hachette UK company

First published in UK 2011 by Hodder Education

This edition published 2011

Copyright © 2011 Tina Konstant

The moral rights of the author have been asserted.

Database right Hodder Education (makers)

Artworks (internal and cover): Peter Lubach
Cover concept design: Two Associates

All rights reserved. No part of this publication may be reproduced, stored in a retrieval system or transmitted in any form or by any means, electronic, mechanical, photocopying, recording or otherwise, without the prior permission in writing of Hodder Education, or as expressly permitted by law, or under terms agreed with the appropriate reprographic rights organization. Enquiries concerning reproduction outside the scope of the above should be sent to the Rights Department, Hodder Education, at the address above.

You must not circulate this book in any other binding or cover and you must impose this same condition on any acquirer.

British Library Cataloguing in Publication Data: a catalogue record for this title is available from the British Library.

10 9 8 7 6 5 4 3 2 1

The publisher has used its best endeavours to ensure that any website addresses referred to in this book are correct and active at the time of going to press. However, the publisher and the author have no responsibility for the websites and can make no guarantee that a site will remain live or that the content will remain relevant, decent or appropriate.

The publisher has made every effort to mark as such all words which it believes to be trademarks. The publisher should also like to make it clear that the presence of a word in the book, whether marked or unmarked, in no way affects its legal status as a trademark.

Every reasonable effort has been made by the publisher to trace the copyright holders of material in this book. Any errors or omissions should be notified in writing to the publisher, who will endeavour to rectify the situation for any reprints and future editions.

Hachette UK's policy is to use papers that are natural, renewable and recyclable products and made from wood grown in sustainable forests. The logging and manufacturing processes are expected to conform to the environmental regulations of the country of origin.

www.hoddereducation.co.uk

Typeset by Stephen Rowling/Springworks

Printed in Spain

MANAGING CHANGE

BULLET GUIDE

Tina Konstant

Acknowledgements

Thanks to all the businesses I've worked with over the years that have contributed to putting this book together.

As always, this is dedicated to Morris!

About the author

Born in Zimbabwe and raised in South Africa, Tina Konstant moved to the UK in 1988. While an undergraduate at the University of Aberdeen, Tina was invited to deliver a series of practical speed-reading workshops to students and the local business community. When she graduated in 1996 she refined and developed the material from the courses to create the speed-reading and information management seminars she delivered to businesses in the private and public sectors. Based on the workshops and consulting projects in the oil and gas sector, she wrote (and continues to write) books on a range of subjects from effective reading and information management to copywriting and change management.

Her debut novel is due out as soon as it's finished!

Contents

1	Recognize the need	1
2	Baby, bathwater and knowing the difference	13
3	So you're going ahead? Who's coming with you?	25
4	Build the plan, then scrap it	37
5	If you can't see it, it's not happening	49
6	The change manager's most useful tool	61
7	When it all goes wrong	73
8	Corrective measures	85
9	The practical psychology of change	97
10	Sustainability	109

Introduction

The first words people utter when the subject of change comes up are invariably that no one likes it. But that's a little like using the weather as an easy topic for small talk – it's a habitual response.

People don't hate change. If we did, we'd never grow up, we'd never learn, we'd never move from job to job or make better friends or better decisions as we grow older. Change is not only inevitable, it's essential. We relish it. It means there's a chance of a bigger, better, brighter future full of hope and potential.

The real issue with change is when it's inflicted on us by *someone else*.

We tend not to mind if change is initiated by a force seemingly outwith our control: weather or random world events. We do mind when another human being takes it upon him- or herself to force us to do or be something other than what we choose at that moment. That is the change we object to and, the truth is, we should.

The reason why it's essential to object to change inflicted upon us by another human being is because, more often than not, the change is not thought through, it's not necessary and there's no guarantee that the outcome is going to be good for us.

The more we resist change in that context, the more it forces thought and careful consideration into the process because, if we didn't resist, people would be demanding us to change at any moment and for any reason.

Saying that, this book is for anyone asking other people to change. So when you meet resistance (and you will) remember why it's happening and be grateful that people respect the change process enough to question it.

1 Recognize the need

The degree of change needed, the complexity of the plan and the challenge you're going to have to achieve buy-in is not in proportion to the size of the change programme but rather to **how much sense it makes to those impacted by it**.

There has to be a need and, more important, the people involved have to recognize it, understand it and accept it.

> **There is nothing more difficult to take in hand, more perilous to conduct, or more uncertain in its success, than to take the lead in the introduction of a new order of things.**
>
> Niccolo Machiavelli

WARNING! Do not manufacture a disaster to force people into change. You want to know why? See Rule of Change No. 6.

When there's trouble, people will accept change that would otherwise be unpalatable. But only if it's real! Don't lie or exaggerate the issue. People will find out and it will lead to disharmony and mistrust.

With this in mind, your first steps towards a successful change management plan must include:

1 Identify the need.
2 Clarify the reasons for change.
3 Know exactly who will be impacted.
4 Do not break Rule of Change No. 1

Rule of Change No. 1: People are not stupid!

Identify the need

Ask yourself …

* How do you like to be treated when change is taking place?
* How do you respond to unnecessary or poorly thought-out change?
* How would you react if instructions to change the way you work came out of nowhere?
* What would your reaction be if the person forcing the change didn't understand what you did?

Before deciding to implement change in any business, no matter how big or small, make sure you:

1 Know why you're doing it.
2 Have the right people to do it.
3 Give your business plenty of warning that it's happening.

To make sure you build a solid foundation for your change programme:

Do

- ✓ Take responsibility for and ownership of the change.
- ✓ Make sure the reason is real, justifiable and understandable.
- ✓ Make sure the company is in a position to take the change.
- ✓ Make sure everyone knows what's happening (even if it doesn't directly impact them).

Don't

- ✗ Pretend global economics or some outside force is responsible for the change.
- ✗ Expect people to change without knowing why.
- ✗ Overload an already overworked team with a change programme – something has to give.
- ✗ Pretend the problem is smaller or bigger than it really is.

Clarify the reasons for change

CASE STUDY

The boss of a mid-size company with huge potential managed to destroy his credibility over just a few short months. This happened because he based the changes he implemented on the books he read. First, leadership was the big thing, and the organization was changed, restructured and redirected accordingly. Then it was six sigma, then blue ocean thinking. The joke in the office centred on what books were found in the toilet – who knew what direction the company was going to take next!

If you're the one deciding on, planning for and rolling out the change, everyone will look to you for two things: (1) the person who can guide them through it; and (2) the person they can blame if it all goes wrong.

Know from the start that you're setting yourself up!

> **TOP TIPS**
> Have good business reasons for change.
> Make sure that the change fits in with what else is going on in the company.
> Make sure that it makes sense!
> When you present the idea to your team, do so with certainty, clarity and confidence but an open mind.
> Listen to the rest of your team. You won't have thought of everything.

Know exactly who will be impacted

Before you design your change management plan, do a full assessment of who will be impacted: not just job roles and departments, but, if possible, the individual people.

No matter how big or small an organization, people will have their own reasons for opting in or out of change. You will know how to persuade people to take part only if you know your audience: their fears, concerns, interests and motivations.

If you ignore people and focus only on what you want to achieve, you will fail – guaranteed and absolutely without question

Key questions to ask people impacted by the change programme you're proposing:

* What is good about how you currently work?
* What isn't working?
* If you could change anything, what would it be?

Let people talk, ramble, complain, moan, disagree and whinge. A single conversation won't get it all out their system, but it will give you a good understanding of how they're feeling and what you need to do to get them on board.

Never break Rule of Change No. 1

People are not stupid!

Always assume that:

* People will always know more than you tell them.
* People will spot a lie and not forget it.
* People are looking for mistakes.
* People will hold you to whatever you put on record.
* People will turn against you if you treat them like idiots.
* People will find the information they need even if you try to hide it.
* People will fill the gaps with theories, ideas and conjecture.
* People will talk to each other.
* People will start rumours.
* People will believe rumours.

Secrets run along two-way streets. If people think you are keeping the truth from them, they will do the same to you.

The real problem that secrets create is that there are a lot more people in the organization than there are in your team, and they can hold back a lot more information than you ever can. If you see any of the following behaviours, then people are probably holding out on you:

* sideways glances and secret smiles during meetings
* people stopping conversations or changing the subject as soon as you walk in
* people agreeing with you in public then not doing what you ask.

2 Baby, bathwater and knowing the difference

This is a mistake that new leaders often make. They think that their presence should be heralded by a clean sweep; anything vaguely tatty should be thrown out. Why? Because it shows they're in command. That they have a plan. That they're better than their predecessor. They're the boss! Aren't they?

Truth is, their colleagues will have already made up their minds and it will be up to the new boss to prove them wrong by carrying out relevant and sustainable change instead of rushing in just to be seen to be doing something.

Rule of Change No. 2: Morale doesn't cost much!

CASE STUDY

A new Chief Executive Officer came into a company in considerable difficulty. The first thing he did was remove towels from the company gym and take away the policy allowing people to do ten days' work in nine. People saw the changes as petty and unfair. The result: alienation and mistrust that took considerable time to overcome.

Lesson to learn?

- Make the right changes first.
- If something works, leave it alone.
- Focus on what hurts people and put that right.
- People don't have to like the change, but it helps if they respect the reasons behind it.

Make sure you're making the right change

Whether you're making changes to the way a small team works or changing an entire organization, check the following before you progress:

1. **The change is needed** Make sure it's not just a case of the new boss/team leader spraying his or her scent over the organization.
2. **The change will have the right impact** If an organization or team is breaking apart, changing the colour of the coffee cups will only irritate people.
3. **Treat the existing systems with respect** Even if it doesn't work well, people will be attached to how they do things. Dismissing existing ways of working is as good as dismissing the people who do the work.

People don't come to work to do a bad job. They do the best they can in the existing environment, so when you outline the reasons for change, *don't make it personal!*

The reason why most businesses go wrong, thus creating the need for change, is because the systems and processes in the business are inefficient and people aren't given the support they need.

> **All is connected ... no one thing can change by itself.**
> Paul Hawken

> **Don't blame the people. You will lose their commitment to the change programme. Look first to the processes and procedures in place**

If something works, leave it alone!

DANGER: If a change is technology related, the mistake project managers make is to force a change because the widget is cool rather than because it will work for the business.

If people are happy working in a certain way and have been for some time, and, more to the point, they are getting results, forcing a change just because it'll look good or because a piece of software exists will not be well received.

If something is already working, prove that the new way of working is better, more efficient, more sustainable or easier – or leave it alone!

Understand the change you're going to make

The only way to implement a solid change programme is to make sure you not only understand where you want the business to go but absolutely understand where it's coming from.

- ☑ Know how the people work.
- ☑ Know the results they need.
- ☑ Know how long it takes to get the job done.
- ☑ Know their problems and challenges.
- ☑ Know what frustrates them about their current processes.
- ☑ Know what works well and what doesn't.
- ☑ Know the people themselves.

The more you know about the job and the business, the more the people will open up and talk to you.

When you gain their trust, they will listen to you too.

Focus on what hurts people and put it right

As soon as change makes people feel better, they'll come on board.

The truth is, people don't mind change. It's the confusion and unknown territory that they object to

The key is to get them through the confusing, unknown territory with as little pain as possible. One way to do that is to find out what hurts them most and fix that.

It's like giving them a boat to sit in as they cross shark-infested water. If the boat leaks, they'll still be scared and confused. If they're in a tanker they won't care so much about the sharks.

How to find out what hurts people most?

Talk to people. Not in a meeting or town hall or environment where they're most likely to keep their thoughts private, but around the coffee machine or the water cooler or in the privacy of their own workspace.

In meetings, people will stay silent or say what they're supposed to say to keep their jobs safe. Around the coffee machine, they're more likely to say what they mean.

People don't have to like the change ...

... but it helps if they respect the reasons behind it.

Don't keep the reason for change a secret. Rule of Change No. 1 is that people aren't stupid, so don't treat them as if they are. Give them the respect they deserve and tell them why the change is happening. You'll be surprised at the amount of help you'll get when people decide for themselves that the change is worthwhile and necessary.

Should you ever keep the reasons for change quiet?

No.

But what if the organization is downsizing and changes need to be put in place to allow that to happen? Isn't it better to keep it quiet then?

No.

The resentment you will generate by lying to people and not giving them the choice will far outweigh the benefit you'll get from being upfront and honest – whatever the consequences.

> **People do have a choice. If they don't like what you're doing, they can leave. You don't have the right to deprive them of the opportunity to make informed decisions**

3 So you're going ahead? Who's coming with you?

Not everyone will agree to a change programme. In fact, before you start, most people will be actively against you. Expect resistance and, if you don't get it, check that you're not alone. People might have left the building without bothering to tell you.

There are four groups of people you need to focus on, each with their own challenges:

1. **The project team driving the change** – their reputation may be at stake.
2. **Leadership** – their bonuses may be at stake.
3. **Middle management** – their careers may be at stake.
4. **Grassroots** – their jobs may be at stake.

CASE STUDY

It takes only one person! At a company carrying out a global change programme, one middle manager who had the ear of the business unit leader representing a third of the business in that region decided the change wasn't good. As a result, the rest of the company underwent the change, but that team didn't. It took three months for the business unit to understand what they were missing. In the meantime, the middle manager had gone on maternity leave and wasn't there to see the consequences of her actions.

Rule of Change No. 3: It takes only one person to block change. Don't underestimate anyone

The project team driving the change

These are the people who will be responsible for running the project and making the change happen. They have a lot invested in the project, and the success or failure of it could impact their careers.

As a change manager you will probably not have been involved in the team selection so you have to work with what you get.

To make change happen, a team needs to feel as if they're being noticed. The best way to do that is to make them visible to the organization.

* Put their names in articles.
* Put their photos on posters.
* Put their biographies on websites.

Don't miss anyone out.

It is vital that each team member is kept informed on what everyone else is doing. If they're not, you'll end up with the project working in silos, resulting in double dipping and inconsistencies. The best way I've come across of keeping the team informed is disarmingly simple.

Get a weekly news brief from each member of the team, collate it into a weekly update and send it to everyone involved in the project.

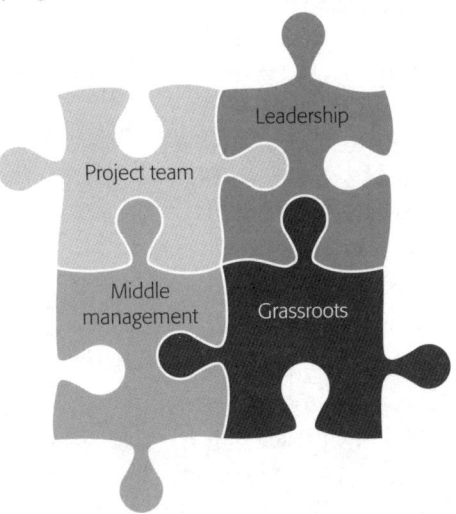

Leadership

The challenge with some leadership teams is that it's not often possible to be fully aware of what motivates them. They could have a personal agenda or, in a big corporation, be driven by senior leadership in another country.

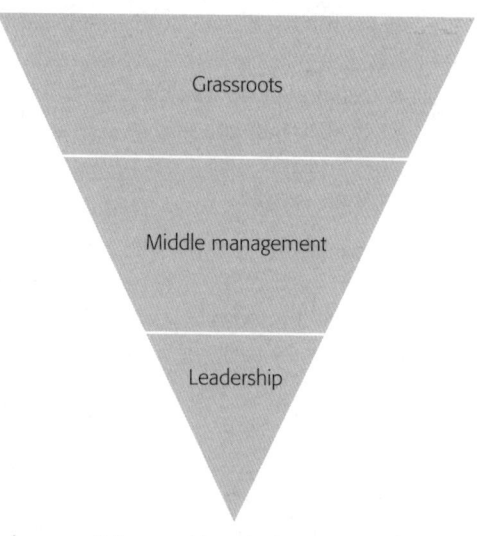

On a very cynical note, leadership sometimes support a project only for as long as it is good for their careers. The change manager needs to be aware of this and monitor the level of their support and what else they're focusing on.

Keep your eyes open for signs that leadership are losing interest in your project. If the leadership team are doing any of the following consistently, then prepare your recovery plan, because you'll need it.

- ☒ start missing meetings
- ☒ delay signing off on agreements
- ☒ avoid you or dismiss updates
- ☒ show little or no interest
- ☒ start pushing other projects forward
- ☒ make things impossible for you by being unnecessarily critical
- ☒ plain and simply won't look you in the eyes.

Unless they come out and tell you they've had a change of heart and can no longer support your project, they'll consciously or unconsciously set you up for failure.

I didn't get to where I am by being nice.

Anon., senior leader of a large corporation

Middle management

This is the most challenging group. These are the people you, the change manager, have to use to get to the grassroots. If your plan doesn't suit their agenda, they'll create an often insurmountable block.

These are the key holders to all the red tape but they're also in the most difficult position. Leadership want to see results. Grassroots want their jobs to be easier. Middle management have to keep both sides happy.

Middle managers who will need your help the most are those who have worked their way up from the grassroots. They would have been people who were so good at what they did that leadership decided they should run the shop. Suddenly you have technical experts asked to chase paper and politics. They get all the work but very little of the satisfaction of actually getting the job done.

> **Stuck behind their desks, gradually gaining weight, middle managers are looking for fun – and messing with your project might just be it!**

Grassroots

These are the people who carry out the day-to-day work. They are practical and will be your greatest allies if the change can be proved to make their lives easier.

However, depending on the business and the project, they may be the most difficult people to reach. They could be offshore, travelling, out on site, with clients or anywhere except in the office and accessible to you.

They're busy with the real work of producing and earning so you have to have something worthy of their attention before they'll give it to you.

1. It has to make sense.
2. It must work.

Getting grassroots on board

The key is getting someone they respect to be your champion

If you have no history or credibility with the grassroots, they won't listen to you. Instead of doing all the talking and being ignored, get someone whose judgement they trust to speak on your behalf or vouch for you. Just like the grassroots, you'll have to do the work to get your champion on board first.

Culture does not change because we desire to change it. Culture changes when the organization is transformed; the culture reflects the realities of people working together every day.

Frances Hesselbein

4 Build the plan, then scrap it

The change management plan must shadow the primary project plan and form the bridge between what changes are needed (people, processes and technology) and the people impacted.

As managing change is all about communication, your plan has to be flexible and open to anyone who wants to add to it.

The plan must be made up of four parts:

* proactive communication
* reactive communication
* emergency communication
* spin.

Rule of Change No. 4: Communicate according to what is needed, not based on a rigid plan

But who likes a plan?

Most people don't like to follow a plan.

The reason for this is because plans are visual reminders of what people said they'd do, what they're yet to do and what they're behind on.

The good news with change management is that you publicize information and updates based on the progress and decisions – whatever they are and whenever they're made:

- ☑ If progress and decisions are made, you can put out good copy.
- ☑ If no progress or decisions are made, you can put out good spin, allowing the team time to get their act together.

The proactive plan

It doesn't really matter what you put down on paper, the important point to get across is that the change management plan can be adhered to only in terms of medium and schedule.

Content can never be predicted because the content depends on what the project does, what decisions are made and how the people respond.

You can plan the media you intend to use and the general dates you will put out communications, but never try to predict content. It might blind you to real progress, which could result in incongruity between what you say is happening and what is really happening.

A proactive plan might look something like this:

	Week 1	Week 2	Week 3	Week 4
Monthly news				▓
Weekly updates	▓	▓	▓	▓
Posters (1)	▓			
Posters (2)				▓
Desk drop			▓	
Open day			▓	
Road show				▓
Leadership visit		▓		
Article (1)	▓			
Article (2)				▓
Milestone update				▓
Intranet go-live	▓			

The reactive plan

No matter how well the project is planned, your change programme will always include a degree of reactive communication.

By *reactive* I don't mean quick and hurried. I mean careful, considered and honest in the face of on-going and current events.

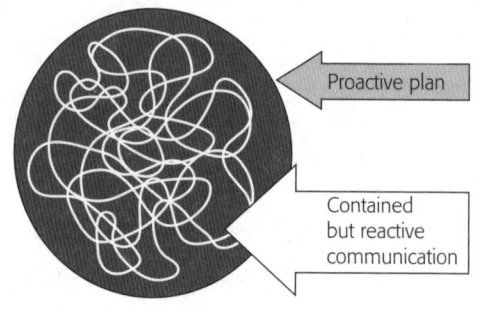

The medium might be planned and proactive but the content is reactive.

It is a bad plan that admits of no modification.

Publilius Syrus, 1st century BC

Reactive communication might include:

1. admitting to mistakes and explaining what's been done to correct them
2. explaining changes in the team and the reasons behind them
3. explaining events that weren't in the plan and the impact they're likely to have
4. explaining any unforeseen change in the plan (content or schedule) and the reasons behind it
5. any event that you think the business will need to hear about that you'd prefer they heard from you first.

Ignore unexpected glitches in project progress and you'll be breaking Rule of Change No. 1 by assuming that people are stupid.

Emergency communication

All your reactive communications can be put out through your proactive plan. Emergency communication, however, needs something special.

In this context, emergency communication doesn't necessarily mean time sensitive. It could be that the message has to get out fast, or perhaps you've already put the message out but people are simply not paying attention to it.

CASE STUDY

In a project recently we had to get a message out, and normal channels weren't working, so we put posters on the back of every toilet door in the building. In less than a week everyone was talking about the project.

If a message is not only time critical, but the content is important too, then you have to consider not only your medium but also **who delivers the message**.

The key is not to be bullied into acting too fast or without carefully considering the details of the message and what impact you want. There are few things worse than putting out an 'urgent' message that does nothing other than create panic.

Spin

Say what you have to say, but say it softly

Unlike the spin we're used to hearing in politics, it's essential that your spin is true. You're telling the truth but putting it in a way that doesn't scare people off.

Tell the truth but don't always tell it.

I don't know who said that first but it's at the heart of good spin.

The real truth behind any change programme is that, if someone doesn't like it, they can pack up and leave. That's the truth. But we're not likely to say it. Instead, we'll give people reasons for change and why they're an important part of the process.

The trouble with spin is that, no matter how you use it, people will still feel manipulated, and they won't thank you for it

The best way to ensure that you maintain your credibility is to use spin only when you have to but, more important, always include the plain truth. If you don't, it'll be Rule of Change No. 1 you'll be breaking all over again …

If people feel that you're not only lying to them but that you also think they're dumb enough to fall for it, then even when you *do* tell the truth (plain and simple), they won't believe or trust you.

5 If you can't see it, it's not happening

Change management is a bit like the proverbial tree being cut in a distant forest; if there's no one there to see it, then it didn't make a sound.

You'll often see change managers working well within a team but not getting a consistent or substantial message out to the workforce. As a result, everyone in the team feels cosy and informed, but the people who need to know what's going on don't know a thing.

The key is to ensure not only that you make a noise, but that you get a noise back.

Feedback from the audience (good or bad) allows you to shape your communication. If you don't get any feedback assume your message is either not being heard or (even more challenging) is being ignored. But how do you know if people are getting your message and, if they are, how they feel about it?

1 Are you being heard?
2 Is your message getting through?
3 Will your message be acted on?
4 Will their actions be the ones you want?

Rule of Change No. 5: Never assume that your message is being heard. Get proof

Are you being heard?

It doesn't matter how much noise you make, if no one hears you, then that's all it is – noise. If all you get back for your efforts are glazed expressions and questions about SpongeBob SquarePants, then you need to stop everything and do the following:

1. Go back to the drawing board and redraft your communication plan.
2. Redefine your message.
3. Review your media.
4. Check that you're speaking to the right people.
5. Start again!

It doesn't matter how far down the road you've gone.
If it's not working, STOP!

Depending on the size of the company, the ideal is to speak to every person one to one and face to face. It's the only guaranteed way of knowing that you're being heard and understood. But, as that isn't always possible, you have to rely on people's actions to know if anyone is paying attention.

You're looking for any response to your message, even if it's people obviously and deliberately trying to avoid you.

Is your message getting through?

> **CASE STUDY**
>
> We put out a company-wide communication for a project that impacted almost everyone. Within minutes of the message going out, someone asked why he should be interested. It was a perfect question that led to a series of clarifying articles and posters informing people why they *should* be interested. That single question told us that we were being heard, but that people weren't getting the message. It totally reshaped our communications approach.

You can have brilliant ideas, but if you can't get them across, your ideas won't get you anywhere.

Lee Iacocca

In that case, we were lucky.

People don't normally like to give feedback because it isn't usually positive and, in most cases, people don't like conflict

Why else shouldn't you expect people to come forward with feedback?

* People don't like putting their heads above the rest. It means that they'll be noticed and, if there are big changes coming, they won't want that.
* People don't like to be publicly negative. They'll complain to friends and colleagues but, as soon as you walk in the room, they'll offer you a cup of tea and talk about the weather.
* People don't like to be the team spokesman.

Will your message be acted on?

So, let's say you've been heard and your message is getting through. Will your message be acted on?

That's the key to change – people DOING something different

Ideally, the first thing you ask people to do should be fairly easy and should take place in no man's land.

That's the primary purpose of training.

Training is an opportunity to get people together to talk about the details of the upcoming change. This environment should provide people with an overview of what's coming as well as time to let the new information sink in.

Using training as part of the change programme

1. Make the first session a workshop instead of one-way training. Let people ask questions (just make sure you have the answers).
2. If possible, allow people to add to, amend and contribute to the training material.
3. Use the sessions to gauge people's moods and attitudes to the change.
4. Never start an argument. Just listen, even if the feedback is negative and forceful.
5. If you promise to take their feedback on board, do so.

The key to using training as a change management exercise is getting people engaged and invested in the programme.

Will the action people take be the right action?

So you've got people in the room, you've had feedback (good and bad), now you need to make sure that they're taking the right action with the right intention behind it.

This will happen only if people fully accept the changes you want to make. If they don't and you force people to change, you are at risk of initiating **malicious obedience**.

This is where people follow your instructions to the letter even (or especially) if they think you're wrong. Then, when it all falls down, they'll blame you.

Bullet Guide: Managing Change

The only way to be certain that people are taking the right action (with the right intention behind it) is to be patient and watch and wait.

People won't immediately change how they work and what they do. It'll be gradual. Give them time and support. Don't leave them alone for a moment.

What you want:

- ☑ people to ask questions
- ☑ people to take it slowly
- ☑ people to think for themselves.

What you don't want:

- ☒ people to be too quiet
- ☒ people to move too fast
- ☒ people to take everything you say literally, without thought.

6 The change manager's most useful tool

It's the job of the *project manager* to know everything that's going on in the project. The trouble is, project managers tend to put out information on a need-to-know basis that could result in people working in isolation from each other.

It is the *change manager's* job to gather information from all parts of the project, condense it in a way that makes sense, and transmit it to everyone within and outside the project team. To do that, a good change manager is professionally nosey.

But there are few rules to stick to:

1. You have to know what to keep a secret and what to tell.
2. Use all feedback – good, bad and indifferent.
3. If you've made a mistake, admit it.
4. Make sure that everything you send out is 100% accurate – your credibility depends on it.

The key is building relationships in which people can talk openly about any aspect of the project, knowing that you'll use only what will do them and the project the greatest service. If any conversation with you comes back to them negatively, they'll never talk to you again.

Rule of Change No. 6: If people don't trust you, they won't believe you

Know what to keep a secret and what to tell

When you're managing change you have to be able to stand on the bridge between the people who want the results and the people impacted. You will be the person both sides want to talk to, and they'll only do that if they trust you to keep their private comments private.

When people open up to you:

Do
- ✔ Listen without criticism or trying to defend the project.
- ✔ Talk like a friend.
- ✔ Be honest about shortcomings.

Don't
- ✘ Defend the project.
- ✘ Repeat what they said when they ask you not to.
- ✘ Ridicule their position or concern.

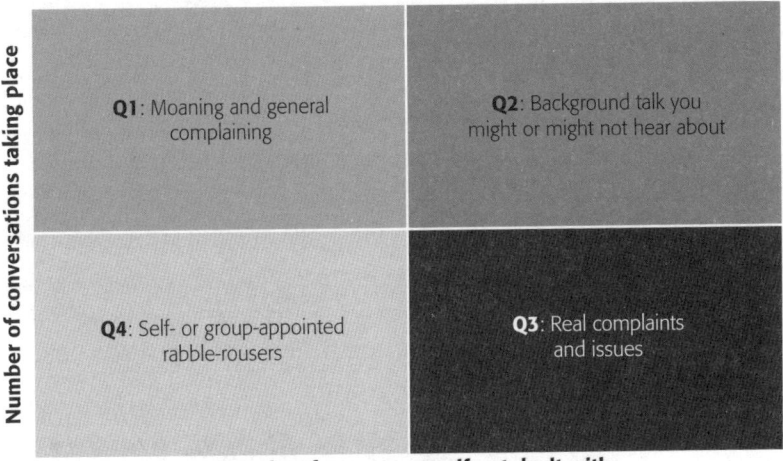

● The four quadrants and the conversations that happen within them

Use all feedback

Now that they're talking, use what you hear!

If you spend your time listening to people and getting to know them and their issues, then you put out communications that seem as if you've not heard them at all, they'll stop talking to you – which is a bad place for someone implementing change to be.

For instance, remember the case study of the man who asked why he should be interested? His comment generated an entire campaign. If we'd done nothing based on his concern, he and others would not have spoken up again.

Use all feedback – good or bad

However ... don't let the tail wag the dog!

If you allow every comment to influence what and how you communicate, the campaign you produce will be disjointed and useless. It's your job to be the filter and decide what goes into print and what remains a conversation.

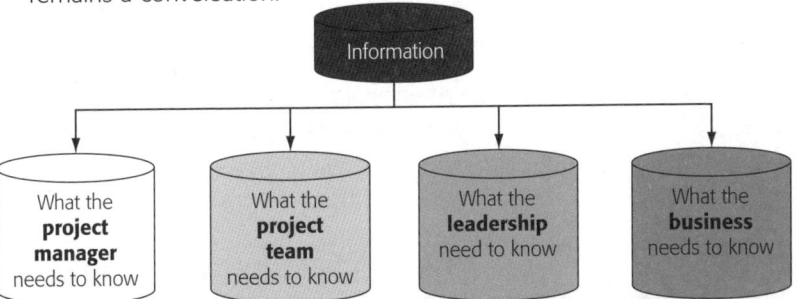

Even those who fancy themselves the most progressive will fight against other kinds of progress, for each of us is convinced that our way is the best way.

Louis L'Amour

If you've made a mistake, admit it

Never lie or try to cover up a mistake – especially if it will impact on the business.

Never. Don't do it. It will always make you look small and desperate.

However, you don't have to tell everything

It's like going to meet your parents-in-law for the first time. You're going to tell them about yourself because they'll want to know, but they don't want to know about all your previous relationships or the last time you got so drunk you couldn't remember how you got home.

Two reasons:

1 There are some things that the business doesn't need to know.
2 It's simply not relevant.

What to admit to
* Issues and concerns that might impact the change programme.
* Decisions that come out of leadership discussions.
* Pending cuts (people and budget).

What you don't have to admit to
* Why specifically people are leaving the project.
* Daily issues and concerns.
* Discussions that haven't been concluded.

The bottom line is that if something is going to impact the project, talk about it

The fact that you're being honest about the bad stuff will tell people that you're being honest about everything, and they're more likely to believe you about the good stuff.

But every time you're going to stand up and confess, think about the parents-in-law.

Make sure that everything is 100% accurate

Check everything. Make sure that every word is accurate and can be backed up.

Writing retractions is a massive time waster and dents the credibility of the project, the team and especially the person who wrote the copy in the first place, so don't put anything out until you're ready.

The core of the project – the discussions, the decisions, the debates and the confusion – are hardly ever revealed to the business. That's background. Your raw material.

Until those conversations are complete, all you can say is, 'Discussions are still in progress.'

Don't pad it out. Don't exaggerate. Don't predict. You never know how the tide will turn.

CASE STUDY

There was a project running in a large organization that touched every part of the business. Communication and PR wasn't the project manager's strong point so she decided that it wasn't necessary to put out any communication about the project. Except for an open day and a few words from the company CEO, there was no update from the team. As a result, after a few months passed the business thought the project was over. In fact, it wasn't even halfway through. What could have been a great project turned into a paper exercise.

For successful change you have to strike the balance between what to tell and what not to tell. Whatever you decide – it has to be accurate

7 When it all goes wrong

A change management programme can go wrong for a number of reasons. You'll only know that something is wrong when you get a response from your audience that you neither want nor expect.

Some of the reasons things might go wrong:

* a change in leadership agendas
* sabotage
* budget cuts and a change in priority
* personal agendas
* boredom resulting from not enough happening soon enough.

Your biggest mistake will be to ignore the signs and pretend that nothing is wrong. At best, your audience will get louder and more belligerent. At worst, they'll ignore you entirely.

Sometimes it's so clear that something is wrong that you feel as if you've been punched in the nose. Other times it's so subtle that you'll hardly notice it all.

Some of the more obvious clues that things are falling apart:

1. refusal to carry out change
2. outright aggression towards you, the project or the team
3. people purposefully undermining the change
4. silence regardless of what you say and do.

Rule of Change No. 7: Know the signs of doom and do something before it's too late – even if it's telling people that trouble is coming

Refusal to carry out the change

The problem

Whether it's one person or the entire organization, this is a serious problem and the biggest sign that the change programme isn't working. It's the equivalent of the workforce going on strike! It can range from people simply refusing to attend training to people point blank refusing to change the way they work. It will stop a project moving forward so it must be addressed.

The solution

You have no choice but to get the key people around a table and talk it through – no matter how rough it gets. This must not just be a public relations exercise. It's gone beyond coffee shop talk. This refusal to take part will affect the business and unless you're the CEO you will not be in a position to tell people to get with the programme or leave. Even if you are the CEO, that kind of threat will break your business.

Ideally, bring in a third party because, at this point, the business will not want to talk to you. **So show a little humility, grow a spine and talk to people.**

Outright aggression

The problem

Most people don't come to work to pick a fight. The only reason rational, calm and productive people bite back is because their jobs, their security, their livelihood, their safety or their reputations are being threatened or undermined.

As shown in Maslow's hierarchy of needs …

The more you take away, the more aggressive people will get.

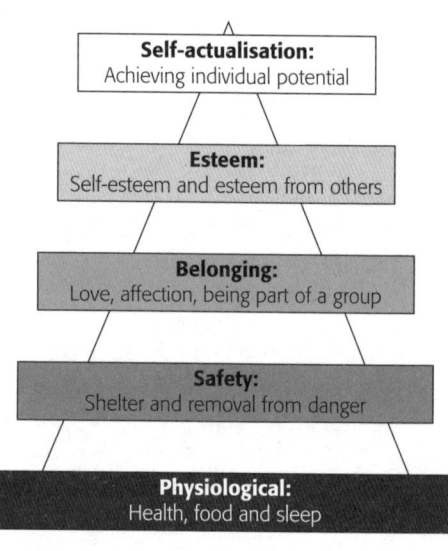

If you want to make enemies, try to change something.
Woodrow Wilson

The solution

When you get people who are normally rational flying off the handle because there's no milk in the company fridge you must listen:

- Don't talk back.
- Don't defend.
- Don't argue.
- Don't get sarcastic.
- Don't justify.
- Don't joke.

It's unlikely that an entire team or business will get violent – unless the business is on the verge of crashing or blanket decisions are being made without consideration of the consequences.

Don't undermine people's frustrations and never patronize them. Keep them talking until you've found what's at the root of their concerns.

People purposefully undermining the change

The problem

If people don't like what's happening but don't have the courage to stand up and say it, they'll try to undermine the project until it fails. Watch out for any of the following:

- ☒ People following new processes and procedures even if they're wrong.
- ☒ People obeying instructions – knowing there's a conflict – but saying nothing regardless of the consequences.
- ☒ People ignoring a dangerous situation but doing nothing about it.
- ☒ People ignoring training and new instructions then making excuses about not hearing or getting the information.
- ☒ People spreading gossip about team members to undermine individuals.

The solution

The undermining of a project or individual will spread virus-like.

It will go something like this:

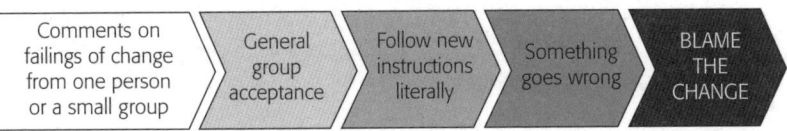

Option 1: Get upset. Tell them what they did wrong and give them corrective action to follow.

Option 2: Take the person aside, find out the root cause if you have to, exclude them from the project.

Silence – regardless of what you say

The problem

The main issue with silence is that you don't have a clue what's really behind it. With every other problem you at least have some idea – even if it turns out to be wrong – of what's going on in people's minds. With silence, you know nothing.

Silence could be good – people are just watching and waiting to see what's going to happen. But it could also be bad – people are watching and waiting to see what's going to go wrong.

It doesn't matter what people are watching and waiting for. If you're going to implement change, it's still a problem because **you need people to talk to you**.

The solution

Get out there and **talk** to everyone. Eventually someone will talk back, even if it's just to shut you up. If people won't accept meetings, get them through every other channel:

- open days
- hijack other meetings
- newsletters
- company news
- posters
- champions
- in the company lift
- coffee machine and water coolers
- through team leaders and bosses
- via email.

Don't stop until someone talks back. Even if they're angry, at least you'll have a conversation.

8 Corrective measures

You're in the middle of meltdown. The reaction you're getting from the business ranges from silence to downright hostility. The team is dealing with facts and figures, while the project manager is dealing with leadership and one-to-one relationships. The person responsible for managing change has to deal with the public at large. At this point the job turns from communications and public relations to facilitation and therapy!

> **Change is hard because people overestimate the value of what they have – and underestimate the value of what they may gain by giving that up.**
>
> James Belasco and Ralph Stayer (*Flight of the Buffalo*, 1994)

To overcome change management challenges:

1. Find out where the noise is coming from.
2. Find out how much influence the people at the root really have.
3. Find the people closest to the root, uncover what they have to lose and get them on board.
4. Deal with the 'blockers' through them.

Most resistance stems from a lack of trust. You need allies. Give them a good reason to be on board. When they're confident, they'll pass the message on a lot more convincingly than you.

Rule of Change No. 8: Never argue your way into people's hearts. It won't work and change won't stick

Find out where the noise is coming from

The person or people at the root of conflict in a change programme are often not the people making the most noise.

It's essential to find out who is at the root. The best way is to talk first to the person standing up front.

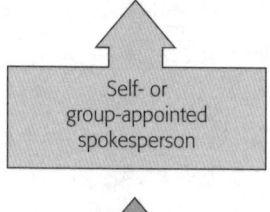

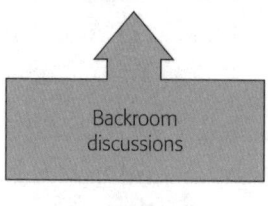

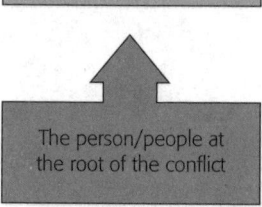

Is this really your idea?

CASE STUDY

A major change was taking place at a refinery. The change wasn't popular and there was a lot of noise. We identified the most vocal rabble-rouser and pulled him aside. After a few detailed questions on why he wasn't happy, it quickly became apparent that he was just the spokesperson: he had a lot of feeling and general opinion but not a lot of detailed knowledge of what people were having difficulty with. It didn't take much for him to start talking about the people standing behind him. These were quieter people who wanted to be heard but didn't want to stand up themselves.

Find out how much influence the people at the root really have

So you've uncovered the real source of contention. It's vital that you do not allow yourself to be intimidated by potential conflict. Before you pay too much attention to the people behind the noise, find out how much influence they really have. Don't look at their job role. That means very little.

Someone at grassroots who has been there a long time will be liked, respected and trusted by his or her team mates. If this person is blocking change, pay attention. He or she can do considerable damage. But don't attempt to deal with 'blockers' directly – you will create a hostile situation.

People hide behind each other when conflict arises. They think there's safety in numbers, but, the truth is, when cuts or changes come, the fallout is felt by each individual, no matter how big a team they are part of. Find out the following:

1. Who will lose out most if the change doesn't happen?
2. In what way will they lose out?
3. What is likely to hurt them most?

> **The key is to get rid of the illusion that stubborn refusal, in the light of a rational need for the business to change, is going to work**

Find people closest to them who have the most to lose

When individuals who have the most to lose recognize that, they'll naturally step away from the crowd and begin to think about themselves first.

Please remember that they will be feeling cornered so don't go scaring them. This isn't about threats and blackmail – it's about people facing the reality of a business in trouble.

Be honest. Tell them exactly what's happening. Give them all the information they need to make an informed decision. Then give them time.

Understand that these people will be taking up an opposite stand to their team mates. They will be putting themselves in a difficult position on your behalf. You need to give them cause to trust you.

Get them on board and give them a great way forward

Once you have these people on board, you have to give them a way forward that makes sense. Be very clear about what you want from them and how they can help themselves and their team. Remember, at this stage they might still be angry, so they really don't care about what the company needs.

What do **they** need?

* training?
* better practices?
* a new role?
* new technology?

Deal with the 'blockers' through your new champions

Once you have one or two people on your road, you need more.

At this point, include the blockers who kicked off the conflict. You've dealt with their issues. You've put changes in place that allow both the business and the people to get what they need.

Champions will be talking to them instead of you. But be careful. Their co-operation is not guaranteed and they will not be thinking of the consequences that their actions will have on the business.

Go back to the case study of the middle manager who blocked a change. Her refusal resulted in everyone in the business, except her unit, working differently …

1. Global reporting couldn't happen because their processes were different, which meant that big bosses abroad very quickly noticed who was out of step. She hadn't thought of that.
2. Working with other units became difficult because they were all working differently. She hadn't thought of that.
3. Communication between units became almost impossible because they were using the same system in different ways. She hadn't thought of that.
4. She was hurting the people she thought she was trying to protect. She hadn't thought of that.

Her team eventually stepped up when they realized that they were becoming too expensive and difficult to run and the business was putting their unit up for sale. She hadn't thought of that.

9 The practical psychology of change

Psychology is full of theories of change: how much people like or don't like it and how they respond to it. But when you're in the thick of managing change, these theories tend to fall down. Perhaps if people read the theory books they'd be more co-operative!

People don't do what's expected of them, and that's what makes change management so challenging and interesting.

The key is engaging people on four fronts:
1. their feelings
2. their thoughts
3. their actions
4. what the business needs.

People's first reaction to change is a feeling (anger, joy, frustration, annoyance, curiosity). Feelings determine thoughts, and thoughts determine actions that are good or bad for the business.

CASE STUDY

A CEO whose company was undergoing change made the mistake of asking people what made them think they had a choice. The company is paying their salary, that's true, but we still live in a democracy and free will is still king, so people will always have a choice, and, if they feel cornered, manipulated or bullied, they will exercise that choice and either sabotage the change or leave the company (and the best people will always go first).

Rule of Change No. 9: Do not assume that everything to do with people is 'soft'. If people are not on board, nothing will happen

Feelings

Whether it's in the office or at home, human beings are governed almost entirely by their emotions.

We make changes in our lives and respond to events around us in a way that will make bad feelings go away and good feelings take their place. It's a fact. It's just how we're wired.

* If our ego is threatened, we'll resist.
* If our feelings are hurt, we'll fight back.
* If people around us make us feel bad, we'll avoid them.
* If we feel overwhelmed, we'll take shortcuts.

IMPORTANT – People's feelings will always make sense to them!

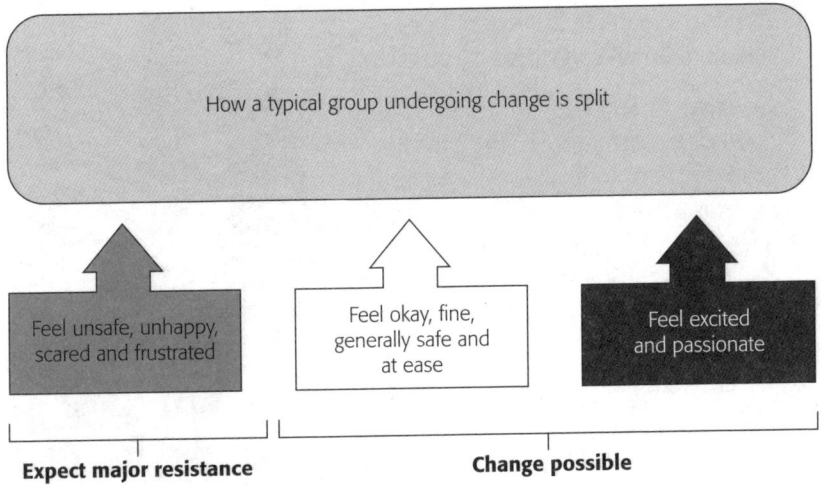

Thoughts

Once you've taken the fear out of a situation, people will need information.

Give them everything they need to understand the reality of the situation, allowing them to finally get rid of any inaccurate preconceptions they might have of what's happening. **Give them the big picture and the details.** Let them ask questions, and give them honest answers. If you don't have all the answers yet, then say so!

CASE STUDY

A business I worked with some time ago had to get rid of more than half its organization. Leadership planted the seed that a sale might be happening then said almost nothing about it for two years. It was mentioned a few times when people asked questions, but all leadership said was yes, at some point it would happen. After two years people had got over their fear of it, they'd thought it through, some had left, most had stayed. When the final announcement was made that they were looking for a buyer, the reaction from most people was 'about time'.

Actions

Finally, you've got people feeling okay about change and they understand what it will take – now you need them to act:

1. Tell them exactly what you want them to do.
2. If they need new skills, provide training.
3. If they need more resources, make sure that they get them.
4. Give them a feedback loop if they have problems.
5. Supply ongoing support for as long as they need it.
6. Deal with issues quickly and visibly.

Why? Because if one person has a problem, others will too. You have their trust, so keep it by being open and transparent.

Eat the frog!

Demonstrate that you and the project are not afraid to do the difficult stuff necessary to drive the change through.

If you hand all the difficult work over to other people to do, then you will never generate the credibility with grassroots to ensure that your change programme is sustained. If there is physical work to do, get in and do it – especially if the business needs extra resources.

Change is good – you go first.
Kenneth F. Murphy

What the business needs

Now that people feel good and they have the information they need and they're taking action, it's time for you to talk to them about what the business needs.

At this point they'll be open to change because it will be clear that what is good for the business is also good for them, and that the people driving the change have considered them and their needs.

If you've done it properly, people will be ready to eat a few frogs themselves to get the job done. They'll do that because they will feel listened to, appreciated and personally invested in the success of the business.

If you don't take care of people's thoughts, feelings and actions ...

Your change programme will fail.

People might allow themselves to be bullied into doing what's good for the business, but the quality of change won't be good and the change won't last. As soon as you turn your back, people will go back to their old ways, laughing about how much of an idiot you turned out to be.

10 Sustainability

You've put something in that works, won people over at every level of the organization, trained everyone who needs it – now don't walk away!

To make sure your project doesn't become another initiative three weeks after the team disbands:

1 Leave support in place – a person (not just a website).
2 Ensure that there is training available for new starts and refresher training for old hands.
3 Ensure that leadership have fully adopted the new way of working, making it 'business as usual'.
4 Keep listening and responding to issues.

Rule of Change No. 10: If you don't mean for the change to last, don't start

The greatest complaint people have at the start of any project? "Why are you wasting time and money? We'll be doing something different in a year."

True. You might be. But, hopefully, what you do next year will be even better, and taking this step right now will allow you to get there.

Nothing is permanent, but change.
Heraclitus, philosopher, 535–475 BCE

No business is static. If it's going to succeed it has to be in perpetual motion. Change will be happening all the time. The key is going back to Chapter 1 and making sure that the change you're making is the right change.

Leave support in place

And make it a person, not a website.

Even if a small piece of information on a website isn't maintained (such as the 'site last updated' details) people will very quickly decide that the whole site isn't current and, within a few months of the project disbanding, they'll go back to their old ways of working.

The minimum human support to leave behind includes:

* a person to talk to when there are questions
* leadership in place who practise what they preach
* a support team to solve technical issues
* a champion to keep the energy going.

The most fragile time in the lifecycle of a project is when it's been disbanded and handed back to the business. It always happens at a time when people are tired and looking for something different. The last thing on their minds is making sure your precious project is sustained. You have to give them every reason to keep going. Stick around and keep them on the road until your way is their way.

Ensure that training is available

CASE STUDY

When budgets are cut, training is often the first to go. A company I worked with found themselves in trouble because they cut their entire support and training division for a piece of software that held their financial processes together. As a result, people did what they could to keep it going, but, after a few years, cracks appeared and the problem resulted in major expenditure to get themselves back on track. If they'd kept training in place, the problem would never have come up. When things are going wrong, training should be the last thing to be cut.

So what should a solid, sustainable training programme include?

1. detailed material that can be used with or without a trainer available to deliver
2. training delivered as part of new-start induction
3. refresher training provided on demand
4. a place where all training material is kept and is easily accessible and controlled
5. someone to go to for help.

Training material must be updated on a regular basis. A business must have someone in place to monitor changes and make sure that training material is updated accordingly. If it isn't, people won't trust it.

Ensure that leadership have fully adopted the new way

Leadership are easily distracted. There is always something new and bigger and more interesting on the horizon. It's their job to look out for it, but the down side is that, when your change programme is over, they'll move on without looking back.

Keep leadership engaged throughout the project so when it's over they have enough of themselves invested to make sure it keeps going

Bullet Guide: Managing Change

It's up to you to guide leadership but it's up to leadership to make sure that the change is sustained in the long term.

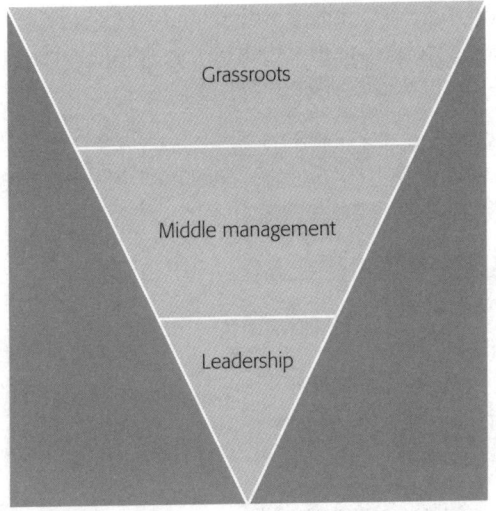

Keep listening and responding to issues

So support is in place, training is kept up to date and leadership are making sure that old habits stay that way – old. How long do you keep listening and responding to issues? For as long as you want people to keep doing what you've asked them to.

Below is what typically happens when the project team breaks up and everyone 'gets back to business'. To avoid it, you have to provide ongoing visible support.

- Support after close-down ↑
- Business engagement →

- Three months after project close-down
- Six months after project close-down
- Nine months after project close-down
- One year after project close-down

Bullet Guide: Managing Change

How do you know you've succeeded?

Say **yes** to the following and you've succeeded in creating sustainable change:

- ☐ Are people happy in their new roles?
- ☐ Are leadership on board?
- ☐ Are you getting feedback from the business?
- ☐ Are people coming to you with new ideas?
- ☐ Are regular communications going out to keep people informed on sustained progress?
- ☐ Has no one threatened or ignored you?

Managing change isn't rocket science – it's all about people, which possibly makes it a little more complicated. To save yourself a lot of hassle and sleepless nights, make sure that you stick to Rule of Change No. 10:

If you don't mean for change to last, don't start!

Further reading

Leading Change by John P. Kotter (Harvard Business School Press, 1996).

What Every Body is Saying: An Ex-FBI Agent's Guide to Speed-reading People by Joe Navarro (HarperCollins Publishers, 2008).

The Art of Profiling: Reading People Right the First Time by Dan Korem (International Focus Press, 1997).

Reading People: How to Understand People and Predict their Behavior – Anytime, Anyplace by Jo-Ellan Dimitrius (Ballantine Books, 1999).

The Art of Speed-reading People by Paul D. Tieger and Barbara Barron-Tieger (Little, Brown and Company, 2006).

There are a number of methods for reading and understanding people and behaviour. In my experience, the most comprehensive, accurate and easiest to apply in the real world is the **Myers–Briggs Type Indicator (MBTI)**. It might take a while to get used to, but I've found it invaluable, even when used at its most basic level.